SUNDAY SUPPERS

MAD HUNGRY

SUNDAY SUPPERS

Go-To Recipes for a
Special Weekend Meal

LUCINDA SCALA QUINN

Artisan | New York

CONTENTS

Sides   56

Desserts   86

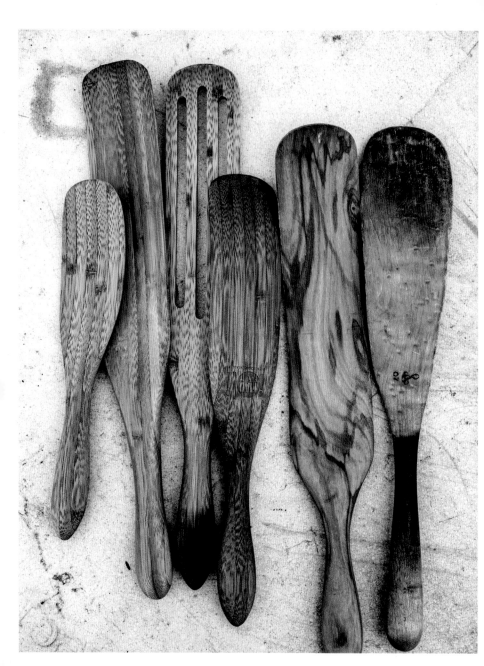

INTRODUCTION

Sunday is the perfect day to spend in the kitchen savoring time with loved ones before the weekend gives way to the Monday-morning work and school routine. Stretch the day by making a memorable dinner that leaves you not just time to enjoy it but maybe some leftovers for lunch or dinner the next day too. Whether you're gathering with your family or friends or both, you can always count on a delicious meal to bring the whole gang together, and with a little planning and dedication, making Sunday supper a regular habit will bring exponential rewards. It's a time to reflect on the past week, set intentions for the week ahead, and take a minute to enjoy each other's company over a satisfying and nourishing meal. Choose a dish like classic Lasagna (page 30), which can be prepared ahead of time and reheated just before dinner, or a long-simmering roast such as Caramelized Orange Pork Roast (page 27) or Luscious Oven-Braised Short Ribs (page 38), which cooks slowly throughout the day, letting its intoxicating scent waft through the house as a pleasant promise of the coming meal.

Once you've gathered—whether you are two or ten—important interactions begin. Around-the-table talk starts with dinner and progresses to sharing thoughts and musings on the day. The dinner table is the first place where our kids gather in a small "community" to express themselves. To talk with and listen to our dining companions is a skill needed for everything we engage in outside the home. Regard eating together as one-stop shopping for wellness. While your body is being fed, your mind and sensory awareness are too. As a regular activity, it's better than pulling the take-out containers (the detritus of which could build a small home) out of the bag and mindlessly chowing down in front of the television. Sure, that can feel liberating now and then—but the next time you do it, ask yourself: Who made this food? Where did it come from? What does the kitchen look like? I guarantee you will not know the answers to any of these questions!

Like any commitment, cooking regularly requires discipline and will. It has to become a priority. It is a challenge to take on, but the rewards are immeasurable. When you make the time to produce a meal at home, it's totally satisfying. We are not too busy to cook! If you can carve out time on a Sunday to landscape your yard, decorate your home, work out at the gym, or practice an instrument, you can cook interesting, healthy food at home on a regular basis.

SHOPPING IS HALF THE JOB OF COOKING

If you keep a well-stocked pantry and tackle any grocery shopping the day before or the morning of, making an extraordinary dinner will be all the more achievable. Plan your shopping ahead of time so you are sure to get all the ingredients necessary for the recipe. Keep your spices stocked and check them for freshness. Put the freezer, the most underutilized appliance in the kitchen, to good use: you will never run out of key ingredients like eggs, butter, or milk. Buy premium meats and poultry, as well as fish of known origins. Onions, garlic, and shallots are your savory saviors for flavor building—keep a full basket in a cool, dark place. Prep fresh vegetables ahead for convenient use: wash, dry, and store salad greens; trim and blanch green beans. Stock your pantry with these staples and supplement for each meal as needed.

DON'T BITE OFF MORE THAN YOU CAN CHEW

Don't tackle too many recipes at once. Start simple. Choose one that engages your interest—for instance, something that you love to eat when you go out, like Chicken Enchiladas Salsa Verde (page 16) or Shrimp Curry (page 50). Then fill out the meal with familiar sides, ones you are used to making. Even the most accomplished cooks I know stick with adding only one or two new things at a time to a routine repertoire.

THINK STRATEGY

Chunk out your time and stay one step ahead. If you're turning on your oven to roast a chicken, roast two: one for dinner and one for sandwiches and soup the next day. Firing up the grill? Make a steak for dinner and grill the vegetables for tomorrow's pasta. Thoughtful meal planning is easier, cheaper, and more wholesome than winging it!

ENLIST FAMILY MEMBERS OR GUESTS TO TAG-TEAM TASKS

Engage your household in the pleasures of cooking and eating good food. First, learn to cook what you love to eat and make it part of your daily routine. Next, involve your family or dinner guests in the process. Make it enjoyable. A shopping trip can be a learning experience for little ones—especially if they're given the opportunity to choose a favorite cereal or ice cream. As soon as they are old enough, give your kids tasks in the kitchen and dining room; everyone will feel good when the food they've worked together to prepare hits the table.

MAINS

vinegar glossed chicken

serves 6 to 8

When rosemary vinegar is added to a pan of golden-brown chicken, alchemy occurs as the vinegar deglazes those brown bits and reduces itself into a syrup. It permeates each chicken piece with an *agrodolce* (sweet-and-sour) flavor. There's no better accompaniment than polenta, soft and loose or firm and sliced. (Rice, pasta, or bread will also work—as long as there is something to sop up the sauce.) This is a dish that only improves when made in advance.

1 cup (240 mL) best-quality red wine vinegar

2 to 3 garlic cloves, minced (about 2 tablespoons)

3 sprigs of fresh rosemary (about 1 tablespoon minced)

5½ pounds (2.5 kg) bone-in chicken pieces (each part should be cut in half)

Coarse salt and freshly ground black pepper

Extra-virgin olive oil

¾ cup (180 mL) chicken broth, plus more as needed

At least 15 minutes but up to 2 hours before cooking, combine the vinegar, garlic, and rosemary to marinate.

Season the chicken pieces with salt and pepper. Heat a 14-inch (36 cm) skillet (or two smaller skillets) over high heat and add a splash of olive oil. Place the chicken in the skillet, skin-side down. Don't crowd the chicken. Work in batches if necessary. You should hear an immediate sizzle when the chicken pieces hit the pan. Don't move them; it takes a couple of minutes to sear the chicken so it doesn't stick. Brown all sides; this will take 10 minutes per batch. Regulate the heat so it stays high but does not burn the chicken. Place all the browned chicken back in the skillet.

Add the chicken broth and scrape up any brown bits from the bottom of the pan. Lower the heat, simmer, and reduce for 15 to 20 minutes. Increase the heat to high and pour in the vinegar mixture. Swirl the pan and stir around as the vinegar evaporates to form a simmering glaze, 8 to 10 minutes. Serve.

chicken parmesan

serves at least 6

You can prepare the sauce and chicken in the morning, then assemble the dish and pop it in the oven just before dinner. With spaghetti, sautéed spinach, and warm, crusty bread, it makes a perfect Sunday dinner.

¼ cup (60 mL) extra-virgin olive oil

2 garlic cloves, minced

Pinch of crushed red pepper flakes

1 (28-ounce/794 g) can tomatoes, lightly pulsed with a blender or food processor

2 teaspoons coarse salt

3 pounds (1.3 kg) boneless, skinless chicken breasts (3 whole breasts, split down the middle)

½ cup (22 g) plain bread crumbs

¾ cup (85 g) freshly grated Parmesan cheese

¼ teaspoon freshly ground black pepper

1 tablespoon unsalted butter, plus more if needed

1½ pounds (680 g) fresh mozzarella cheese, sliced thin

Heat a saucepan over medium-high heat and add 1 tablespoon of the olive oil, the garlic, and the red pepper flakes. Stir for 30 seconds. Add the tomatoes and ½ teaspoon of the salt. Simmer for 30 minutes.

Meanwhile, working on a large surface covered in baking parchment or plastic wrap, lay down the chicken breasts. Using a sharp slicing knife, cut each piece in half horizontally through the middle.

In a large prep pan or dish, combine the bread crumbs and ½ cup (60 g) of the Parmesan cheese. Spread out to cover the whole bottom of the pan. Lay down as many chicken breasts as will fit on the mixture. Sprinkle salt and pepper over each piece and turn over, completely coating them with the bread crumb mixture. Repeat the process with the remaining pieces of chicken.

Heat a large skillet over medium-high heat. Swirl in 2 tablespoons of olive oil, along with the butter, to coat the pan. Add the chicken breasts in one layer and cook until golden, about 3 minutes on each side. Remove and repeat the process for the remaining chicken, adding a little oil and butter to the pan as needed.

Preheat the oven to 400°F (200°C). Spoon some tomato sauce into a greased 9 by 13-inch (23 by 33 cm) baking dish to cover. Layer in the chicken pieces and top with mozzarella slices. Spoon over about 1¼ cups (300 mL) more sauce and sprinkle on the remaining ¼ cup (25 g) Parmesan cheese. Bake until golden and bubbling, 30 to 35 minutes. Let rest for at least 15 minutes before serving.

chicken enchiladas salsa verde

serves 6

If you're pressed for time, use a store-bought green sauce (made from tomatillos) and shredded store-bought rotisserie chicken for a quicker version of this dish. These bubbling, subtle-tasting enchiladas are even better with a cool, crunchy salad on top.

GREEN SAUCE

½ white onion, peeled and coarsely chopped

2 garlic cloves, unpeeled

2 serrano or jalapeño chiles, stems removed

14 whole tomatillos, peeled and simmered in water for 5 minutes

¼ cup (38 g) unsalted roasted peanuts

2 teaspoons coarse salt

½ cup (120 mL) chicken broth

ENCHILADAS

1 tablespoon vegetable oil, plus 2 teaspoons more for dressing the salad

3 cups (720 mL) green sauce

12 corn tortillas, toasted, stacked, and wrapped in a clean kitchen towel to steam

4 cups (600 g) shredded chicken (from a 3-pound/1.4 kg poached chicken)

1⅓ cups (7 ounces/200 g) crumbled queso fresco, or shredded Monterey Jack cheese

3 to 4 cups (84 to 112 g) shredded romaine lettuce, washed and dried

6 radishes, trimmed and sliced

1 teaspoon white vinegar

Coarse salt and freshly ground black pepper

continued

To make the sauce, preheat the broiler. Place the onion, garlic, and chiles on a baking sheet. Broil for 4 minutes, or until charred and blistered. Discard the garlic skin. Place the onion, garlic, and chiles in a blender jar with the tomatillos, peanuts, salt, and broth. Blend until smooth.

Preheat the oven to 375°F (190°C).

To make the enchiladas, heat a saucepan to medium-high and add the tablespoon of oil. Carefully pour in the green sauce and cook, stirring constantly, to thicken up, about 3 minutes. One by one, dip the tortillas in the sauce, place in an ungreased 9 by 13-inch (23 by 33 cm) baking dish, fill with some chicken, and roll up. Fit each enchilada snugly next to the other in the baking dish. Pour the remaining green sauce over the enchiladas. Sprinkle the cheese on top. Bake for 15 minutes, or until the sauce is bubbling and the enchiladas are heated through.

Meanwhile, toss the lettuce and radishes with the remaining 2 teaspoons oil, the vinegar, and salt and pepper. Layer the salad on top of the hot enchiladas and serve immediately.

flat roast chicken

A roast chicken or two is a wonderful way to feed a horde of ravenous guests or family members. Laying the whole bird flat allows it to cook in under an hour. Gone is the problem of the breast cooking before the rest; all the pieces cook evenly. If you wish, finish with a sauce poured over after cooking, which tastes tangy and delicious over the crisp skin. An ovenproof 14-inch (36 cm) skillet, preferably cast-iron, makes for an easy job.

1 whole chicken, 3 to 4 pounds (1.4 to 1.8 kg), backbone removed

Coarse salt and freshly ground black pepper

¼ cup (60 mL) extra-virgin olive oil

2 tablespoons unsalted butter

3 tablespoons fresh lemon juice

¼ teaspoon crushed red pepper flakes (optional)

2 garlic cloves, smashed and peeled (optional)

Preheat the oven to 425°F (220°C). Place the chicken on a cutting board. Using kitchen shears, cut along one side of the backbone. Open the chicken's legs and spread the bird down flat, skin-side up. Press down firmly on the breastbone to flatten it. Pat it dry with paper towels. Salt and pepper generously on both sides.

Heat a large ovenproof skillet, such as cast-iron, on high heat. Add 1 tablespoon of the olive oil and 1 tablespoon of the butter. Immediately add the chicken, skin-side down.

Allow to brown (without moving) for 3 minutes.

Turn the chicken over, careful not to break the skin, and transfer the skillet to the oven.

The chicken is done when it is golden brown and cooked through, 40 to 45 minutes. An instant-read thermometer inserted in the thickest part, not touching bone, should read 165°F (74°C). Remove the chicken to a cutting board to rest for 10 minutes. Add 1 tablespoon of the lemon juice

and the remaining tablespoon of butter to the pan drippings and swirl around.

Meanwhile, if you want to make the lemon sauce, whisk together the remaining 3 tablespoons olive oil, 2 tablespoons lemon juice, the red pepper flakes, garlic, and a pinch of salt. Cut the chicken into pieces, drizzle with the pan sauce and the optional fresh lemon sauce, and serve immediately.

Roasting pan method: Follow the first step, then place the chicken in a large, shallow roasting pan, skin-side up, and put in the oven. Proceed to the third step and complete.

FLAT ROAST CHICKEN RIFFS

Tangy—Season the bird on both sides with salt (plenty of it) and pepper. Cook as directed. Swirl some fresh orange juice and butter into the pan drippings at the end.

Earthy—Add paprika to the salt-and-pepper mix to burnish the bird with an auburn hue. Cook as directed.

Spicy—Mix a teaspoon of garam masala (an Indian spice mix) with the salt and pepper, adding a little more salt than usual to balance the sweet spices. Cook as directed.

Garlicky—After browning the bird on the skin side, flip it over and snuggle several smashed garlic cloves under the carcass (instead of the citrus). They will lightly perfume the bird and enhance the flavor of the pan juices. Add a few sprigs of fresh herbs to the garlic pile, such as rosemary, sage, or oregano.

BBQ-y—Generously season the bird on both sides with salt and pepper. Set up the grill for indirect heat. Place the chicken skin-side up on the side without fire. Cover the grill and open the vents. Cook for 45 minutes. Brush with your favorite barbecue sauce. Turn the bird over onto the fire side of the grill to crisp the skin (taking care not to burn), about 5 minutes. Brush sauce on the underside of the bird and flip to cook underside for 1 minute. Let rest for 10 minutes before cutting. Serve with extra barbecue sauce.

chicken tikka masala

serves 6

Chicken tikka masala, the most famous of all Indian dishes, constitutes an entire food genre all its own. This recipe takes inspiration from several traditional dishes and turns it all into one delicious hybrid. For a complete Indian feast, serve with rice, a bowl of cool thick yogurt, some store-bought mango chutney, and Indian naan bread.

12 boneless, skinless chicken thighs

Coarse salt and freshly ground black pepper

2 tablespoons safflower oil

1 small onion, chopped

3 garlic cloves, minced

1 (1-inch/3 cm) piece ginger, peeled and finely grated

1 small green chile, such as serrano

1 tablespoon ground cumin

¼ teaspoon cayenne pepper

2 tablespoons garam masala

1 (28-ounce/794 g) can tomato puree

½ cup (120 mL) water

¼ cup (60 mL) heavy cream

Season the chicken with salt and pepper. Heat a large skillet over medium-high heat. Add the oil. When it shimmers, add the chicken to the hot pan and brown on both sides for about 3 minutes. (Work in batches if necessary.)

Transfer the chicken to a plate and add the onions, garlic, and ginger to the pan. Cut a slit into the chile lengthwise and add to the pan. Sauté until the onions and garlic are softened, 3 to 5 minutes. Add the cumin, cayenne, and garam masala and cook for 30 seconds.

Add the tomato puree and water and stir. Add the chicken and bring to a simmer, then cover and simmer, turning the chicken occasionally, until it is cooked through and the sauce has thickened, about 30 minutes. (The dish can be made ahead to this point.)

Stir in the cream and simmer for 1 minute. Serve.

pork chops with apples and onions

serves 6

This simple dish is easy to vary: replace the onions with leeks or add a sliced potato, and deglaze the pan with beer, white wine, chicken broth, or water. A big pot of rice, a couple of vegetables, and you have a generous and filling dinner.

6 bone-in pork chops (loin or shoulder), cut ¾ inch (2 cm) thick

Coarse salt and freshly ground black pepper

1 tablespoon extra-virgin olive oil or vegetable oil

2 tablespoons unsalted butter

1 large white onion, sliced

2 to 3 apples, cored and sliced (about 3 cups/342 g)

1 cup (240 mL) beer, white wine, cider, or chicken broth

Trim the chops of excess fat. Sprinkle generously with salt and pepper on both sides. Heat a 14-inch (36 cm) cast-iron skillet (if you have a smaller one, you'll need to work in batches) over high heat, and then swirl in the olive oil. Lay in the pork chops and don't move them for a few minutes to ensure that a good, golden sear forms. Turn and brown well on the second side for a total of about 10 minutes. Remove the chops to a warm plate.

Swirl the butter into the pan. Add the onion and apples. Sauté until the onion slices are lightly caramelized and the apples have begun to soften, about 8 minutes. Stir in the beer or other liquid. Return the chops to the pan.

Cook until the pork is tender, about 15 more minutes (depending on the size of the chops), turning halfway through and covering the chops with the apple mixture. If the apple mixture needs a little thickening, remove the chops to the warm plate again and simmer the mixture on high for a few minutes to reduce. Serve the chops over rice or mashed potatoes with a large spoonful of the apple-onion mixture over the top.

caramelized orange pork roast

serves 10 to 12

This pork roast marinates and cooks in the same delicious sauce for 5 hours—low and slow in the oven—but don't be turned off by the long cooking time; it needs no babysitting. It's essential not to undercook the roast, but overcooking it is practically impossible.

1 cup (240 mL) white wine

1 cup (240 mL) soy sauce

¾ cup (163 g) brown sugar

½ cup (120 mL) Sriracha hot sauce

⅓ cup (75 g) whole-grain mustard

¼ cup (60 mL) rice wine vinegar

Finely grated zest and juice (about ½ cup/120 mL) of 1 large orange

6 garlic cloves, minced

1 (6- to 8-pound /2.7 to 3.6 kg) bone-in pork shoulder (if skin-on, score in a crosshatch pattern)

Whisk together all the ingredients except the pork in a large roasting pan. Poke the pork all over and place in the pan with the marinade. Turn the meat several times while it marinates in the refrigerator for at least 4 hours or overnight.

Preheat the oven to 325°F (165°C). Loosely tent the roasting pan with foil and cook the marinated pork for 1 hour per pound. Every hour, drizzle the meat with the pan sauce and add ½ cup (120 mL) water as needed throughout to prevent the sauce from becoming too concentrated and scorching in the pan.

Remove the foil. If the pork is caramelized at this point, continue cooking at 325°F (165°C); if not, raise the heat to 375°F (190°C). Cook until an instant-read thermometer reads 190°F/88°C (the point at which the cartilage melts), about 1 hour more, basting the pork with the pan sauce a few more times.

Remove the roast from the oven. Let rest for 20 minutes. Shred or slice the meat and return it to the pan with the sauce. Serve with extra sauce.

green pork chili

serves 8 to 10

This chili is a revelation—spicy and deeply wholesome, with an unmatched yin-yang combination of herbaceous chiles and soft, savory meat. A large bone-in pork shoulder (or butt or picnic ham) remains a total bargain for feeding a group. If you want to save time on the prep work at home, ask the butcher to remove the bone and cube the meat for you.

4 pounds (1.8 kg) boned pork shoulder, cut into 1½-inch (4 cm) cubes

Coarse salt

2 tablespoons vegetable oil

3 large onions (preferably white), chopped

1 whole head garlic, peeled and minced

12 green chiles (such as Hatch, Anaheim, or poblano), roasted, peeled (optional), seeded, and chopped into 1-inch (3 cm) squares

6 cups (1.4 L) chicken or pork broth

10 flour tortillas, warmed

Heat a large Dutch oven or other heavy-bottomed pot over medium-high heat. Coat the meat with a generous amount of salt. Swirl the oil into the pot. When it shimmers, work in batches to brown the meat on all sides, 6 to 8 minutes per batch.

Transfer the browned meat to a plate. Remove excess fat from the pot, leaving behind about 2 tablespoons. Add the onions and garlic to the pot. Sauté until softened, about 3 minutes, scraping up the browned bits on the bottom of the pan. Add the chiles, stir to combine, and cook until softened, about 5 minutes more.

Return the meat to the pot and pour in the broth. Add 2 teaspoons salt. Bring to a boil, then partially cover, reduce the heat, and simmer, stirring occasionally, until the pork is almost tender, about 1½ hours. Remove the lid and continue to simmer until the liquid has thickened a little and the meat is tender, about 1 hour more. Season with salt to taste and serve with warm flour tortillas.

lasagna

makes 12 large servings

This lasagna feeds five or six for dinner, including seconds, and is still delicious reheated the next day. Stash it in the freezer and you'll never be left unprepared to feed a mass of people. It goes straight from freezer to oven, but add 20 minutes to the cooking time.

1 pound (454 g) lasagna noodles or packaged precooked lasagna noodles

Coarse salt

5 links sweet Italian sausage, or a mixture of hot and sweet, pierced with a fork

1 large egg

1¾ cups (1 pound/454 g) ricotta cheese

¾ cup (85 g) freshly grated Pecorino Romano or Parmesan cheese, plus more for serving

5 cups (1.2 L) Basic Italian Tomato Sauce (recipe follows)

1 pound (454 g) fresh or prepackaged mozzarella cheese, cut crosswise into ⅓-inch-thick (8 mm) slices

Extra-virgin olive oil, for drizzling

Bring a large pot of water to a boil over high heat. Add the noodles and a generous pinch of salt and cook for half as long as the package suggests. Drain and float in cold water. (Skip this step if noodles are precooked.)

Preheat the oven to 350°F (180°C). In a medium skillet over medium-high heat, fry the sausage links until cooked through, about 10 minutes. With kitchen scissors, cut the sausage into disks in the pan and continue to fry over low heat until the cut surfaces are crispy, about 20 minutes. Drain off the fat.

In a medium bowl, stir together the egg, ricotta, and ½ cup (60 g) of the Pecorino.

To assemble the lasagna, spread 1 cup (240 mL) of the tomato sauce in the bottom of a greased 9 by 13-inch (23 by 33 cm) baking dish. Drain and pat dry the noodles. Overlap one third of the noodles atop the sauce to cover the pan bottom. Spread all the cooked sausage over the noodles and spoon over another cup (240 mL) of sauce. Lay down the second third of noodles. Evenly dollop all the ricotta mixture on top of the noodles and flatten with the spoon to make an even layer. Top with the remaining noodles to completely cover the cheese. Pour over 1½ to 2 cups (360 to 480 mL) sauce to cover. Evenly lay all the mozzarella slices on top. Sprinkle around the remaining ¼ cup (30 g) Pecorino and drizzle with olive oil.

Bake uncovered for 40 minutes, or until the lasagna is bubbling all over and lightly golden on top. Let rest for 10 to 15 minutes before slicing. Serve with grated cheese and warmed extra sauce at the table.

basic italian tomato sauce

makes 3 cups (720 ml)

1½ tablespoons extra-virgin olive oil

2 garlic cloves, minced

⅛ teaspoon crushed red pepper flakes

1 (28-ounce/794 g) can best-quality tomatoes, pulsed with a blender

½ teaspoon coarse salt

1 sprig of fresh basil (optional)

1 tablespoon unsalted butter (optional)

Heat a medium saucepan over medium heat. Swirl around the olive oil to coat the pan and when the oil is hot, add the garlic and red pepper flakes. Stir constantly for 30 seconds, just long enough to release the garlic's fragrance and transform it slightly from its raw state. Don't cook it to golden.

Raise the heat to high and stir in the tomatoes and salt. Bring to a boil, reduce the heat, and simmer, uncovered, for 30 minutes. In the last 5 minutes of cooking, add the basil sprig, if using. Remove the basil before serving and swirl in the butter, if using.

meatballs and tomato sauce

The type of meat you use for these meatballs is up to you (all beef, half beef/half pork, part veal), but whatever your preference, start with 2 pounds (1 kg) of ground meat. If spaghetti and meatballs are for dinner, you'd better have made enough for seconds, late-night raids, and leftovers. The meatballs freeze beautifully in the sauce.

⅓ cup (80 mL) milk

2 slices best-quality bread, crusts removed

1 pound (454 g) ground pork

1 pound (454 g) ground beef

2 garlic cloves, minced

2 tablespoons minced onion

2 large eggs, lightly beaten

¾ cup (85 g) grated Pecorino Romano cheese, plus more for serving

2 tablespoons chopped fresh parsley leaves

¼ teaspoon freshly ground black pepper

½ teaspoon coarse salt

2 tablespoons extra-virgin olive oil

2 (28-ounce/794 g) cans best-quality whole tomatoes, pulsed with juices with a blender

Freshly grated Parmesan cheese, for serving (optional)

In a small saucepan, heat the milk. Soak the bread in the milk, turning the slices over to absorb it. Cool and mince the bread. Place it in a large bowl. Add the meats, garlic, onion, eggs, cheese, parsley, pepper, and salt. Using clean hands, mix together until completely combined.

Have a rimmed baking sheet or platter ready. If you have time, chill the raw meatballs to firm them up. Roll into 1½-inch (4 cm) meatballs. (If you periodically run cold water over your hands, the meat won't stick to them as you roll.)

Heat a 14-inch (36 cm) skillet (or two smaller skillets to fry in batches) over high heat. Add the olive oil and when it is very hot, add the meatballs in a single layer. Don't crowd the pan; work in batches if necessary. Fry the

meatballs without moving for a few minutes, then turn as they cook to brown on all sides, 8 to 10 minutes. Spoon out any excess oil from the pan, carefully scraping around the meatballs.

Add the tomatoes and scrape the bottom of the pan to incorporate all the browned bits. Simmer for 30 minutes. Serve hot pasta with 3 meatballs on top, some sauce, the grated cheese, and freshly ground black pepper.

shepherd's pie

serves 6

Shepherd's pie brings the classic combination of meat and potatoes together in just one bite by topping flavorful ground meat with a creamy, baked potato mash. Save on dishes by sautéing the meat mixture in the same oven-safe, deep skillet you will bake the pie in. Alternatively, sauté the meat in a skillet and assemble the pie in a separate casserole dish.

5 medium potatoes, such as Idaho or russet, peeled and roughly chopped into 2-inch pieces

Coarse salt

8 tablespoons (1 stick/113 g) unsalted butter

2 carrots, chopped

1 celery stalk, chopped

1 large onion, finely chopped

2 pounds (1 kg) ground lamb or beef, or a combo

¼ cup (60 mL) Worcestershire sauce

Freshly ground black pepper

¾ cup (180 mL) chicken or beef broth

2 teaspoons cornstarch

½ cup (120 mL) milk, plus more if needed

1 cup (160 g) frozen peas, thawed and drained

Place the potatoes in a large pot and add enough cold water to cover by 2 inches (5 cm). Add a generous amount of coarse salt. Bring to a boil and cook until tender enough to mash, 15 to 20 minutes.

Preheat the oven to 400°F (200°C).

Meanwhile, melt 2 tablespoons of the butter in a 10-inch (25 cm) oven-safe skillet (preferably cast-iron) over medium-high heat. Add the carrots, celery, and half the onion and sauté until softened, about 4 minutes. Add the meat and 2 teaspoons salt and cook over high heat, pressing and stirring to break up the meat, until the moisture has evaporated and the meat is browning in fat, about 15 minutes. (The skillet will seem overly full, but the mixture will cook down.) When the meat is browned, stir in the Worcestershire sauce and cook for 1 minute.

continued

Whisk together the broth and cornstarch in a small bowl and add to the meat mixture. Simmer for an additional minute to thicken.

Drain the potatoes, setting aside ½ cup (120 mL) of the cooking water. Return the potatoes to the pot. Add the reserved cooking water, milk, and 4 tablespoons (57 g) of the butter and season with pepper. Mash until smooth. Add more milk if needed to achieve a smooth, spreadable texture.

Spread the meat mixture around in the bottom of the pan it was cooked in or transfer to a 2-quart (2 L) casserole dish. Evenly distribute the peas and remaining onion over the meat. Dollop and spread the mashed potatoes over the vegetables. Dot the top of the potatoes with the remaining 2 tablespoons butter.

Bake until heated through, the potatoes are golden on top, and the filling is bubbling, about 30 minutes.

steak pizzaiola

serves 6 to 8

The aroma of this steak cooking in the caramelized, tomatoey sauce is indescribably inviting and memorable. The whole thing is cooked in one large ovenproof skillet, which works its magic untended once it is placed in the oven. Serve with bread or polenta and sautéed Swiss chard on the side. Or, present it as a "sauce," with all the meat shredded uniformly and tossed with a pound of big pasta such as rigatoni and a fluffy cloud of grated Parmesan cheese on top.

2½ pounds (1.1 kg) bone-in chuck steak, or 2 pounds if boneless

1 teaspoon coarse salt

Freshly ground black pepper

2 tablespoons extra-virgin olive oil

3 to 4 garlic cloves, minced

1 teaspoon dried oregano

1 teaspoon dried thyme

¼ teaspoon crushed red pepper flakes

1 tablespoon tomato paste

1 (28-ounce/794 g) can whole tomatoes, with juice

NOTE

The secret of this dish is to use fatty meat with big bones, such as chuck steak, one of the most affordable and flavorful cuts of meat you can buy. It's browned first, then slowly simmered in liquid until it becomes meltingly tender.

Preheat the oven to 325°F (165°C). Season the meat on both sides with salt and pepper. Heat a large ovenproof skillet over high heat and swirl in the olive oil. Brown the meat on both sides. Remove the meat from the skillet and take the pan off the heat.

Stir into the pan the garlic, oregano, thyme, red pepper flakes, tomato paste, and whole tomatoes. Mash up the tomatoes with the back of a spoon, return the meat to the pan, spoon the sauce over it, and cover tightly.

Braise in the oven for at least 2 hours, stirring occasionally. Uncover and cook for an additional 30 minutes, until the sauce has thickened up.

luscious oven-braised short ribs

serves 6

Most recipes for short ribs tell you to brown the meat on the stove top before adding the braising liquid and cooking it. This recipe doesn't, eliminating the mess, time, and attention that this step requires. Add the potatoes in the last 45 minutes, or omit them and serve the ribs with noodles, rice, or polenta if you prefer.

1 onion, finely sliced

4 garlic cloves, smashed

1 leek, cleaned and finely chopped

1 carrot, finely chopped

1 celery stalk, finely chopped

4 sprigs of fresh thyme, or 1 teaspoon dried thyme

1 cup (240 mL) red wine

½ cup (120 mL) soy sauce or tamari

1 tablespoon sugar

¼ teaspoon freshly ground black pepper

3½ pounds (1.6 kg) short ribs

2 to 3 Idaho potatoes, peeled and cut in quarters (optional)

Mix all the ingredients except the meat and potatoes in a 9 by 15-inch (23 by 38 cm) roasting pan. Add the ribs and rub all over with the marinade. The meat should fit comfortably in a single layer in the pan. Cover and let marinate in the refrigerator for 6 hours or up to overnight. Occasionally turn the meat over in the marinade. Remove from the refrigerator 30 minutes prior to cooking.

Preheat the oven to 400°F (200°C). Braise the short ribs (covered) for 2½ to 3 hours total, reducing the heat to 350°F (180°C) after an hour. Turn the ribs over. Uncover and add the potatoes in the last 40 minutes of cooking. Add water to the pan if too much liquid evaporates. You want to end up with glistening ribs in a reduced glaze.

butterfield stageline chili

serves 6 to 8

This chili stands out because of the ground pork and cubed beef brisket combination, which brings a fantastic texture, chew, and mouthfeel to the chili. If you don't have the time or patience to prep your meat as the recipe instructs, ask your butcher to do so.

4 pounds (1.8 kg) beef brisket, cut into ½-inch (1 cm) pieces

1 tablespoon plus 1 teaspoon coarse salt

½ teaspoon freshly ground black pepper

¼ cup (60 mL) extra-virgin olive oil

2 pounds (1 kg) ground pork

2 large white onions, chopped

4 Anaheim, Hatch, or poblano chiles (6 ounces/170 g), chopped

1 Scotch bonnet or habañero chile, minced (seeds and ribs removed for less heat, if desired)

6 garlic cloves, minced

2 tablespoons tomato paste

2 tablespoons chopped fresh oregano

3 tablespoons chili powder

1 tablespoon ground cumin

2 (28-ounce/794 g) cans whole plum tomatoes in juice

2 cups (480 mL) chicken broth

Season the brisket with the salt and pepper. Heat a Dutch oven over medium-high heat. Add 2 tablespoons of the oil and when it shimmers, add half the brisket.

Brown, turning occasionally, for 4 to 5 minutes; transfer to a plate. Repeat with the remaining brisket.

Add the remaining 2 tablespoons oil to the pot, then add the pork, onions, chiles, and garlic and cook, stirring occasionally, until the pork is no longer pink and most of the liquid has evaporated, 6 to 8 minutes.

Stir in the tomato paste, oregano, chili powder, and cumin and cook for 2 minutes, until fragrant.

Puree 1 can (28 ounces/794 g) of the tomatoes with a blender and stir into the chili, along with the remaining tomatoes and the chicken broth. Return the brisket to the pot. Bring to a boil, cover, reduce the heat, and simmer, stirring occasionally, until the beef is fork-tender, 3 to 3½ hours. Ladle into bowls and serve.

tamale pie

This recipe does away with the labor intensity of individual tamale prep. All the components of a good tamale are here, layered together in a large group-friendly casserole. Think of it like a Mexican-style shepherd's pie.

2 tablespoons extra-virgin olive oil

1 medium yellow onion, chopped

1 green bell pepper, cored, seeded, and chopped

2 teaspoons coarse salt

1 tablespoon chopped fresh oregano or 2 teaspoons dried

1 teaspoon ground cumin

1/4 teaspoon freshly ground black pepper

1 pound (454 g) ground beef chuck

1 tablespoon tomato paste

1 (14½-ounce/439 g) can whole plum tomatoes

2½ cups (600 mL) water

1 cup (134 g) fine cornmeal

3/4 cup (3 ounces/85 g) grated Monterey Jack cheese

1 jalapeño, minced

2 ears yellow corn, kernels and milk stripped from cobs, or 1½ cups (248 g) frozen corn kernels

Preheat the oven to 375°F (190°C) with a rack in the center position. Heat a 10-inch (25 cm) cast-iron skillet over medium-high heat. Add the oil to the pan. When the oil shimmers, add the onions, bell pepper, and 1 teaspoon of the salt and cook until the vegetables are soft and golden in places, about 5 minutes.

Add the oregano, cumin, pepper, and ground beef and cook, stirring, just until the beef is cooked through, 4 to 5 minutes. Stir in the tomato paste and cook for 1 minute. Add the tomatoes, breaking them up with the side of the spoon, and simmer until the mixture is slightly thickened, about 5 minutes. Remove from the heat.

Bring the water to a boil in a medium saucepan. Stir in the cornmeal and the remaining teaspoon of salt and cook, stirring until thick and creamy, 2 minutes. Remove from the heat and stir in the cheese, jalapeño, and corn. Spread evenly over the beef mixture.

Transfer the pan to the oven and bake for 40 to 45 minutes, until the top is golden and the filling is bubbling around the edges of the pan. Let stand for 20 minutes before serving.

basic beef stew

serves 10 to 12, or 6 for one meal,
with leftovers to freeze for another

Achieving a deep rich flavor in a basic beef stew depends upon browning the meat. It takes a little extra time and attention, so why not double your efforts and prepare enough to feed a large crowd, or freeze half the batch for another meal. Once the dark golden sear is achieved on the meat and the herbs are sautéed, the stew simmers away unattended on the stove.

5 large carrots, peeled (2 finely diced, 3 cut into ¾-inch/2 cm chunks)

4 celery stalks (2 finely diced, 2 sliced crosswise into ¼-inch/6 mm slices)

6 medium potatoes, peeled and cut into 1½-inch (4 cm) chunks

4 pounds (1.8 kg) beef, cut into 2-inch (5 cm) chunks (use chuck steak or half chuck/half bottom round)

Coarse salt and freshly ground black pepper

2 tablespoons vegetable oil

¼ cup (33 g) all-purpose flour, for dredging

1 tablespoon unsalted butter

2 onions, chopped

4 garlic cloves, minced

2 tablespoons tomato paste

3 sprigs of fresh thyme, or 1½ teaspoons dried thyme

½ cup (120 mL) red wine (optional)

8 cups (2 L) beef or chicken broth

1 tablespoon hot red pepper sauce (optional)

Float the carrot, celery, and potato chunks in a large bowl of cold water until needed.

Toss the meat with a generous amount of salt and pepper. Heat a large Dutch oven or other heavy-bottomed pot over medium-high heat. Swirl the oil into the pot. Working in batches, coat the meat pieces in flour and add to the pot. Brown on all sides, 8 to 10 minutes, then transfer the browned meat to a plate. Repeat until all the meat is browned, adding more oil if necessary.

Pour off all but a few tablespoons of fat. Swirl in the butter. Add the onions, garlic, diced carrots, and diced celery. Cook on medium-low heat until lightly caramelized, 10 to 12 minutes. Stir in the tomato paste and thyme and cook for 2 more minutes.

Raise the heat to high. Add the wine, if using (or ½ cup/120 mL of broth), and stir to deglaze the pan, scraping up the browned bits stuck to the bottom. Return the meat to the pan and add the broth, which should cover the meat (add water if necessary). Bring to a boil, then reduce the heat to low, cover, and simmer for 2 hours.

Drain the carrot chunks, celery slices, and potato chunks. Add to the pot and cook until tender, 30 to 35 minutes. Remove 4 potato pieces, then mash them and stir back into the stew to slightly thicken the mixture. Stir in the hot sauce, if using. Taste and add more salt if necessary. Serve hot. (To freeze: Cool the stew and store in an airtight plastic container in the freezer for up to 3 months.)

BROWNING MEAT

The mantra: Don't crowd the pan. Make sure your pan is very hot before you add the (preferably room-temperature) meat pieces; leave enough room surrounding each piece in the pan so air can circulate around the meat as it browns. Don't move the pieces for a few minutes as the sear sets in. Turn and repeat the process on all sides of the meat. It's the browned bits on the bottom of the pan, known as the "fond," that form the basis for the flavor of the stewy sauce. If you crowd the pieces together in the pan, the meat will steam as all the liquid releases instead of browning.

standing rib roast

serves 10 to 12

The hardest part of this recipe is the price of the meat. Do not be surprised if it runs you $15 to $20 a pound. The ribs form their own rack, so all that's needed is a nice sturdy roasting pan or a large pan with 2-inch-tall sides. I always serve this with prepared horseradish on the table.

1 (4- to 6-rib) beef roast, trimmed, at room temperature (it will take at least an hour out of the refrigerator)

2 tablespoons dry or Dijon mustard

2 tablespoons sugar

2 teaspoons coarse salt

1 teaspoon freshly ground black pepper

Extra-virgin olive oil

Preheat the oven to 450°F (230°C) with the rack in the lower third of the oven. Lightly score the fat on top of the meat in a diamond pattern. Place in a roasting pan, rib-side down. Combine the mustard, sugar, salt, and pepper and rub the mixture all over the meat. If need be, mix another batch of the dry rub in order to fully coat the meat. Drizzle a little oil over the top of the meat and pour enough water into the bottom of the pan to reach a depth of ¼ inch (6 mm) (this prevents smoking).

Place the roast in the oven. After 15 minutes, reduce the heat to 375°F (190°C) and continue to roast, basting frequently, until an instant-read thermometer registers between 125 and 130°F (52 and 54°C) for medium-rare, about 1 hour and 45 minutes. Start checking the temperature of the meat after 1 hour; the meat will cook quickly during the last half hour. Total cooking time is about 2 hours for a 5-rib roast.

Transfer the roast to a cutting board, tented loosely with foil, for at least 20 minutes (the internal temperature should rise to 135°F/57°C). Reserve the pan juices for gravy, and the fat for Yorkshire Pudding (page 84). Use a very sharp knife to carve the meat.

KILLER GRAVY

Place the roasting pan across two burners over medium heat. Combine ½ cup (120 mL) beef broth and ¼ cup (33 g) all-purpose flour in a lidded jar and shake until well combined. Slowly whisk the flour mixture into the pan, scraping up the browned bits, and cook until thick and bubbling, about 2 minutes. Slowly add a little less than 4 cups/1 L stock to the pan, whisk to combine, and simmer until slightly thickened, about 5 minutes. Strain if too lumpy.

roast leg of lamb
with lemon, garlic, and oregano

serves 6 to 8

Make sure to plan ahead with this one, because this recipe starts by marinating the lamb in a seasoning paste for as long as possible, anywhere from 1 to 24 hours—the longer the better. (This is a fantastic paste to use on roast chicken, too.) The meat cooks beautifully both in the oven and on the grill.

2 whole lemons, washed, seeded, and chopped

2 sprigs of fresh rosemary, leaves removed

5 to 6 garlic cloves, peeled

1 tablespoon coarse salt

½ teaspoon freshly ground black pepper

2 to 4 tablespoons extra-virgin olive oil

1 boneless leg of lamb, butterflied, boned, and cut to lay flat (about 5 pounds/2.2 kg)

Place the chopped lemon, rosemary, garlic, salt, pepper, and olive oil in a food processor. A blender can also be used, if done in batches. If you have neither, finely chop all the ingredients together.

Open up the lamb and lay it flat. Spread and massage the lemon paste evenly over the inside and outside of the lamb. Place in a baking dish and cover, or place in a large resealable plastic bag. Refrigerate overnight to marinate, turning occasionally.

Preheat the oven to 450°F (230°C). Remove the meat from the refrigerator 30 to 60 minutes before cooking. Place the lamb on a rack in a foil-lined roasting pan or rimmed baking sheet. Place the meat in the oven and after 5 minutes, reduce the temperature to 425°F (220°C). Roast for 45 minutes, or until medium rare, 140°F (60°C) on an instant-read thermometer. Allow the meat to rest for 10 to 15 minutes before carving and serving.

shrimp curry

serves 4 to 6

Keep a jar of store-bought curry paste on hand so that you can easily throw together this traditional Thai-style curry in under 30 minutes. Use this recipe as a basic guideline; add whichever vegetables are available, swap out shrimp for shredded chicken or pork, or keep it vegetarian without any meat at all. Serve it with rice or rice noodles.

2 tablespoons vegetable oil

3 celery stalks, thinly sliced

2 bell peppers, red and/or green, cored, seeded, and sliced

3 Thai chiles or other small hot chiles, seeded (if concerned about heat) and minced

4 garlic cloves, minced

1 shallot, minced

2 inches (5 cm) of fresh ginger, peeled and grated

Coarse salt

3 tablespoons red curry paste

2 (14-ounce/400 mL) cans coconut milk

2 tablespoons fish sauce

1 pound (454 g) shrimp, peeled

Freshly ground black pepper

Crushed red pepper flakes

1 head broccoli, cut into florets

4 cups (696 g) cooked rice, or 8 ounces (227 g) rice noodles, cooked, for serving

1 cup (40 g) roughly chopped fresh cilantro leaves, for serving

1 lime, cut into wedges, for serving

Heat a shallow braising pan over medium-high heat and swirl in 1 tablespoon of the oil. Stir in the celery, bell peppers, chiles, garlic, shallot, ginger, and a pinch of salt and cook, stirring continuously, until softened, 1 to 2 minutes.

Lower the heat to medium and stir in the curry paste to combine with the vegetables. Cook for about 2 minutes. Pour in the coconut milk and fish sauce and let simmer, partially covered, for about 15 minutes.

Meanwhile, pat the shrimp dry with a towel and season all over with salt, black pepper, and red pepper flakes. Heat a large sauté pan over high heat. Swirl in the remaining tablespoon of oil and add the shrimp in a single layer. Sear the shrimp on one side, without moving, until golden brown, about 1½ minutes.

Add the broccoli to the coconut curry mixture, then add the shrimp. Increase the heat to high, cover, and cook until the shrimp is opaque and the broccoli is tender, about 5 minutes. Serve the shrimp in bowls over rice or noodles, garnished with the chopped cilantro and lime wedges.

seafood paella

serves 4 to 6

Paella is a Spanish dish of saffron-scented rice, meat, and seafood that is prepared all in one pot. Making it gives you a chance to use linguiça, a delicious Portuguese sausage. It will feed a hungry group with no more than a simple green salad and loaf of bread.

Two 1½-pound (680 g) lobsters

4½ teaspoons extra-virgin olive oil

1 small yellow onion, peeled and chopped

1 red bell pepper, cored, seeded, and diced

2 links linguiça (about ½ pound/227 g), skinned and chopped; or chopped cured Spanish-style chorizo or other cured sausage

2 cups (370 g) white rice

3 cups (710 mL) fish or chicken broth, heated

1 pinch of crushed saffron

Coarse salt (depends on saltiness of linguiça and clams)

1 dozen littleneck clams, well cleaned

1½ pounds (680 g) codfish or any firm-fleshed white fish, cut into 2-inch pieces

Sprigs of fresh parsley, coarsely chopped, for garnish

Bring 1½ inches (4 cm) of water to a boil in a large stockpot. Add the lobsters, cover, and cook for 13 minutes. Remove the lobsters and cool just enough to handle. Crack the shells and remove the meat. Keep the claws whole and chop the remainder of the meat into large pieces and reserve.

Preheat the oven to 450°F (230°C). Heat a 12-inch (30 cm) ovenproof skillet or paella pan over medium-high heat. Add the olive oil and sauté the onion and bell pepper until the onion is translucent, about 5 minutes. Add the linguiça and cook for 3 minutes. Gently stir in the rice and cook for a few minutes to lightly toast.

Add the broth, saffron, and salt and bring to a boil over high heat. Remove from the heat and cover with a lid or with a sheet of foil and place the paella in the oven for

10 minutes. Uncover and scatter the clams around on top of the rice. Cover and cook for 15 minutes more, or until the clams are open and the liquid is absorbed. With 3 minutes left to cook, add the codfish and lobster. Discard any clams that do not open. Garnish with parsley and serve.

eggplant parmesan

serves 8

This is a baked Eggplant Parmesan—unconventional for a dish that is usually fried, but so much easier. Like the fried version, though, this dish delivers that longed-for crusty, cheesy eggplant flavor.

4 medium eggplants (about 1 pound/ 454 g each), sliced crosswise into ⅔-inch-thick (1.5 cm) slices

Coarse salt

2 tablespoons extra-virgin olive oil, plus more for drizzling

4 garlic cloves, minced

2 (28-ounce/794 g) cans whole tomatoes, pulsed with a blender

½ teaspoon crushed red pepper flakes

6 cups (258 g) fresh bread crumbs

2 cups (240 g) grated Parmesan cheese, plus more for topping

4 large eggs

2 cups (260 g) all-purpose flour

2 (8-ounce/227 g) balls fresh mozzarella cheese, sliced

Freshly ground black pepper

Season the eggplant slices all over with salt and arrange on 2 baking sheets. To make the tomato sauce: Heat a large saucepan over medium-high heat. Swirl in the oil. When it shimmers, add the garlic and sauté, stirring, for 30 seconds. Stir in the tomatoes and red pepper flakes. Simmer for 30 minutes.

Combine the bread crumbs and cheese in a shallow dish. Whisk the eggs with a pinch of salt in another dish. Spread the flour in a third dish. Using a clean cloth towel or paper towel, press down on both sides of the eggplant slices to remove the moisture created by the salting process. Ready a couple of clean baking sheets (top with a wire cooling rack if you can) before beginning the breading process.

Preheat the oven to 400°F (200°C). Using a fork or tongs, dip each slice of eggplant (on both sides) in the flour, then in the eggs, and finally in the bread crumbs. Lay each piece on the baking sheets and let the breaded slices rest to dry out for 10 to 15 minutes. Bake until a deep golden crust forms, 30 to 40 minutes. Reduce the heat to 375°F (190°C).

Spread a thin layer of the tomato sauce on the bottom of a 9 by 13-inch (23 by 33 cm) baking pan. Arrange some of the eggplant slices to cover the bottom of the pan. Top each piece of eggplant with 1 slice of mozzarella and then spoon a little tomato sauce over the mozzarella. Continue layering with the remaining ingredients. Spoon a thin layer of tomato sauce over the top layer and sprinkle with Parmesan cheese and freshly ground pepper. Drizzle with oil and bake until golden brown and bubbling, 30 to 35 minutes.

SIDES

cranberry-almond green salad with honey mustard vinaigrette

serves 4

Toasted nuts and sweet-tart dried fruit—these are the two fairy godmother ingredients that transform a plate of raw vegetables into something you are dying to eat.

1 head Boston lettuce, torn into bite-size pieces

¼ cup (21 g) sliced almonds, toasted

¼ cup (32 g) dried red cranberries

HONEY MUSTARD VINAIGRETTE

¾ cup (180 mL) olive oil

2 tablespoons freshly squeezed lemon juice (about ½ large lemon)

2 teaspoons Dijon mustard

½ teaspoon honey

Coarse salt and freshly ground black pepper

½ cup (2 ounces/60 g) blue cheese (optional)

Combine the lettuce, almonds, and cranberries in a large salad bowl.

Make the vinaigrette: In a jar with a tight-fitting lid, combine the oil, lemon juice, mustard, and honey. Cover tightly and shake well to combine and emulsify. Season with salt and pepper and shake again before serving.

Pour the dressing over the salad and toss to coat. Crumble blue cheese on top, if desired.

iceberg and endive wedges with blue cheese vinaigrette

serves 2

This is a wonderful "grown-up" version of your classic, run-of-the-mill, bottled-blue-cheese-dressing iceberg wedge salad.

1 head iceberg lettuce, cut into wedges

3 Belgian endives, cut lengthwise into quarters, leaving the core end intact

½ cup (2 ounces/60 g) creamy blue cheese

¼ cup (60 mL) red wine vinegar

⅓ cup (80 mL) extra-virgin olive oil

¼ teaspoon freshly ground black pepper

Arrange the iceberg wedges and endive on a platter.

Crumble the blue cheese into a jar. Using a fork, smash up the cheese a little bit. Add the vinegar, olive oil, and pepper, put the lid on the jar, and shake the dressing until combined and creamy.

Pour a few tablespoons of the dressing over the salad and serve. Store the extra dressing in the refrigerator for up to 2 weeks.

escarole walnut salad

serves 6

If you've never worked with escarole, give this versatile green a go. In this recipe, toasted walnuts, homemade walnut oil, red wine vinegar, and shavings of Pecorino nicely balance escarole's healthful, raw intensity.

2 cups (228 g) walnuts

½ cup (120 mL) extra-virgin olive oil

1 garlic clove, smashed

¼ cup (60 mL) red wine vinegar

½ teaspoon coarse salt

¼ teaspoon freshly ground black pepper

1 head escarole, chopped

½ small red onion, thinly sliced

¾ cup (3 ounces/85 g) shaved Pecorino Romano cheese

Preheat the oven to 350°F (180°C). Spread 1 cup (114 g) of the walnuts on a rimmed baking sheet and toast in the oven for 10 minutes. Turn the nuts once during roasting. Cool to room temperature and coarsely chop.

Finely chop the remaining 1 cup (114 g) walnuts and place in a small saucepan with the olive oil and garlic. Bring to a bare simmer over medium heat. Remove the pan from the heat and set aside to cool to room temperature. When cool, strain the oil into a medium bowl and discard the nuts and garlic. Whisk in the vinegar, salt, and pepper.

Spread the escarole over a large platter. Sprinkle the toasted walnuts and onions over the escarole and drizzle with the dressing. Top with the shaved Pecorino Romano and serve immediately.

kale salad

The beauty of this recipe is that, unlike most salads, it benefits from being made ahead. The hearty, tenacious greens relax and soak up the lemony dressing—making it great for dinner parties at a friend's or when your main course will need all your attention before you sit down to eat.

Finely grated zest and juice (about 5 tablespoons/75 mL) of 1 large lemon, plus more juice if needed

½ teaspoon coarse salt

¼ teaspoon freshly ground black pepper

½ cup (120 mL) extra-virgin olive oil

1 small bunch kale, tough stems removed, leaves finely sliced crosswise (about 6 cups/126 g), chilled

1 cup (120 g) grated Pecorino Romano or Parmesan cheese, or a combo of the two

1 cup (85 g) sliced or slivered almonds, toasted

Whisk together the lemon zest and juice, salt, and pepper in a small bowl. Slowly pour in the oil, whisking continuously to emulsify the dressing.

Combine the kale and cheese in a large bowl. Drizzle the dressing over the salad and toss to fully coat the leaves. Press and massage the greens slightly in the process. With a wooden spoon, stir in the almonds and season with more salt and lemon juice, if needed. This recipe can be made ahead (up to 8 hours before serving) and refrigerated until you're ready to eat.

white bean salad

Once you make a batch of this salad, you'll find yourself using it for many different meals. If it's made in advance, the taste only improves. Feel free to vary the herbs to best accent the protein you're serving this with—adding mint if served with lamb, dill with fish, basil with roast chicken.

3 (15-ounce/425 g) cans cannellini beans, drained

½ cup (60 g) chopped red onion

½ cup (20 g) chopped fresh parsley leaves

¼ cup (10 g) chopped or torn fresh dill, mint, or basil (optional)

½ teaspoon coarse salt

¼ teaspoon freshly ground black pepper

1 recipe Rose's Vinaigrette (recipe follows)

3 scallions (green part only), finely sliced

Combine the beans in a large bowl with the red onion, parsley, optional herb of choice, salt, and pepper.

Slowly stir in the vinaigrette to taste. Garnish with the scallions. Serve immediately or refrigerate. The salad will keep in the fridge for up to 3 days.

rose's vinaigrette

makes 1 cup (240 ml)

1 tablespoon minced shallot or garlic

1 teaspoon Dijon mustard

1 teaspoon light brown sugar

¾ teaspoon coarse salt

¼ teaspoon freshly ground black pepper

¼ teaspoon Worcestershire sauce

2½ tablespoons red wine vinegar

2 tablespoons fresh lemon juice (about ½ large lemon)

¾ cup (180 mL) extra-virgin olive oil

In the bottom of a clean jar, mash together the shallot, mustard, brown sugar, salt, pepper, and Worcestershire sauce.

Pour in the vinegar, lemon juice, and olive oil. Cover tightly and shake well to combine and emulsify. Add salt and pepper to taste. Use immediately or store in the refrigerator.

oven-roasted vegetables

The keys to perfect oven-roasted vegetables are to cook at a high oven temperature and to be generous with the olive oil, salt, and pepper. If you're cooking different types of vegetables, make sure the sizes and textures are similar so they're all done at the same time.

1 bunch of small carrots, peeled

4 medium beets, cleaned, trimmed, and quartered

8 ounces (227 g) cremini mushrooms, trimmed and wiped clean, large ones halved

5 shallots, peeled and halved

¼ cup (60 mL) extra-virgin olive oil

1 tablespoon coarse salt

Coarsely ground black pepper

Preheat the oven to 400°F (200°C). Place each type of vegetable in its own area on a rimmed baking sheet. Drizzle the olive oil over all the vegetables. Sprinkle with the salt and pepper.

Roast until the vegetables are tender and lightly caramelized, 25 to 30 minutes. Test each type of vegetable for doneness. Arrange on a serving platter.

OTHER VEGETABLES TO OVEN-ROAST

Brussels sprouts—The best! Cut in half, lengthwise.

Asparagus—Snap off the fibrous ends.

Broccoli—It works, but I prefer it steamed.

Any root vegetable—Clean, cube, and season well.

Scallions—Trim both ends and roast whole.

Onions—Peel and slice or quarter.

Potatoes—Small new potatoes can be whole or halved. Cut large potatoes crosswise into ¼-inch (6 mm) slices.

char-baked tomato, zucchini, and eggplant

serves 6 to 8

This is the dish to try if you think you don't like zucchini or eggplant. Critical to the success of this dish is to bake it way longer than you expect and keep pushing down the mixture with a spatula to release the moisture. By the time it is done, the vegetables will be thoroughly caramelized, soft and luscious, and the dish will be easy to cut into wedges or squares.

⅓ cup (80 mL) extra-virgin olive oil

1 onion, peeled and sliced

5 small tomatoes, thinly sliced

Coarse salt and freshly ground black pepper

1 small eggplant, about 6 inches (15 cm) long, thinly sliced crosswise

2 zucchini, about 5 inches (13 cm) long, thinly sliced lengthwise

2 garlic cloves, thinly sliced

½ teaspoon fresh thyme leaves

Preheat the oven to 400°F (200°C).

Pour some of the olive oil to cover the bottom of a 9 by 13-inch (23 by 33 cm) rectangular or 12-inch (30 cm) oval baking dish. Layer in half the onion slices and one third of the tomatoes. Generously sprinkle with salt and pepper. Add a layer of eggplant and sprinkle on more salt. Add another third of the tomatoes, the zucchini, garlic, thyme, and the remaining onions. Top with the remaining tomatoes. Press down on the mixture with your hands. Pour over the remaining olive oil. Season generously with salt and pepper. (Don't worry. The vegetables will be piled high but collapse as they cook.)

Bake uncovered for 1½ hours. After 45 minutes, press the mixture down firmly with a spatula. The vegetables should be reduced in height, and should be brownish black and caramelized, almost charred in places. Return to the oven to finish roasting. Let cool for at least 10 minutes, so the mixture can solidify a bit. Cut into squares and serve.

creamed spinach

serves 6

This tender spinach, suspended in a light, silky, creamy cloud, is reminiscent of Stouffer's popular frozen creamed spinach. Clean and steam the spinach in advance, make the béchamel (white sauce), fold it all together at the last minute, and heat it through.

2½ pounds (1.1 kg) fresh spinach, washed, water still clinging to the leaves

3 tablespoons unsalted butter

¼ cup (33 g) all-purpose flour

1 cup (240 mL) milk

1 teaspoon coarse salt

Pinch of freshly ground black pepper

Pinch of ground nutmeg

Steam the spinach in a large pot for 2 to 4 minutes, just until the leaves have all collapsed. The water clinging to the leaves will be enough to cook it. Drain, cool, and squeeze out the liquid in a strainer. Coarsely chop the spinach.

To make the béchamel, heat a sauté pan over medium heat, and then melt the butter and whisk in the flour. Cook, stirring, for 1 minute. Whisk in the milk until fully incorporated and simmer for 30 seconds. Stir in the salt, pepper, and nutmeg.

Fold in the spinach and serve immediately.

stuffed artichokes

These artichokes will feel like a special dish worth serving for a holiday or celebration. The key is to use high-quality bread crumbs and a good Italian grating cheese. If you don't have Pecorino Romano, you can easily substitute with Parmesan or try a mix of the two.

1 lemon, halved

6 whole artichokes

¾ cup (32 g) fresh bread crumbs

½ cup (60 g) grated Pecorino Romano cheese

1 small garlic clove, minced

2 tablespoons chopped fresh parsley leaves

Freshly ground black pepper

Squeeze the lemon halves into a large bowl and fill the bowl with cold water. Trim the bottom off each artichoke. Trim off the tough outer leaves. Snip the thorny tips off the top leaves. As each one is completed, place it in the lemon water to prevent it from discoloring.

In a small bowl, combine the bread crumbs, cheese, garlic, and parsley and season with pepper. Pull each leaf open slightly from each artichoke and stuff a little filling into the openings. Place the artichokes snugly side by side in a large pan with a tight-fitting lid. Add 1 inch (3 cm) of water to the pot. Cover, bring to a boil, then reduce the heat and steam until the bottoms of the artichokes are tender, 35 to 45 minutes; a knife should insert easily. Make sure the water doesn't boil dry. Add more water if necessary.

Serve each artichoke hot, on an individual plate.

MAKING HOMEMADE BREAD CRUMBS

There is no reason to pay for premade, store-bought bread crumbs, which usually lack flavor and texture. Whether you use fresh loaves or packaged sliced bread at home daily, accumulate the ends in a bag and freeze. When you have collected enough and have some extra time, break it into pieces using a knife or your bare hands and place in a food processor or blender jar. Pulse to the desired crumb size; generally I shoot for a resemblance to grains of rice. The results are better if done in small batches. To make by hand, place dry bread in a sealed bag. Smash with a rolling pin to break into crumbs. Place in a resealable bag and store in the refrigerator for up to 1 month. If using fresh bread, place slices on a baking sheet and dry out slightly in a 300°F (150°C) oven for 15 minutes. Cool and prepare as directed. You can store these in the freezer for up to 3 months.

sautéed asparagus
with shaved parmesan

serves 6

A fresh, simple preparation that you'll find in a legit Italian trattoria during asparagus season, or displayed in a gourmet food case any time of year.

2 tablespoons extra-virgin olive oil

2 pounds (1 kg) asparagus, ends trimmed and cut on the bias into 2-inch (5 cm) pieces

1 teaspoon coarse salt

Rounded ¼ teaspoon freshly ground black pepper

1 teaspoon grated orange zest (about 1 small orange)

Juice of 1 large orange (about ½ cup/120 mL)

¾ cup (3 ounces/85 g) shaved Parmesan cheese, or to taste

Heat a large skillet over high heat. Add the oil. When it shimmers, add the asparagus, salt, and pepper and sauté, stirring frequently, until the asparagus is crisp-tender, about 3 minutes. Stir in the orange zest and cook for 1 minute. Add the orange juice and stir a few times.

Transfer to a serving platter and scatter the Parmesan over the top. Serve immediately.

maple-thyme roasted carrots

serves 4 to 6

Carrots adapt to many different cooking techniques, making excellent sides for meats and poultry. Maple syrup and thyme accentuate their natural sweet flavor.

2 tablespoons extra-virgin olive oil

2 tablespoons maple syrup

Leaves from 3 thyme sprigs

½ teaspoon coarse salt

1 pound (454 g) carrots, peeled and sliced on the bias

Preheat the oven to 400°F (200°C) with a rack in the upper-third position. Mix the olive oil, maple syrup, thyme, and salt together in a medium bowl. Add the carrots and toss to coat.

Spread the carrots on a small baking sheet or in an ovenproof skillet and roast for 20 minutes, until tender and golden on the edges. Serve warm.

steamed yet crispy string beans

Green beans feel like one of the more "meaty" vegetables (especially with the addition of thinly sliced prosciutto!), so this dish works well as a side with a vegetarian pasta or meatless main.

1 pound (454 g) haricots verts or green beans, halved lengthwise

1½ to 2 tablespoons olive oil

4 slices prosciutto, ham, or salami, thinly sliced crosswise

3 jarred roasted red peppers, drained and minced

½ teaspoon coarse salt

¼ teaspoon crushed red pepper flakes

Bring ¼ inch (6 mm) of water to a boil in a large skillet. Add the beans, cover, and steam until tender, 3 to 4 minutes. Drain the beans and wipe the pan clean.

Heat the skillet over medium heat. Swirl in 1 tablespoon of the oil. When it shimmers, add the prosciutto and sauté until crispy, about 2 minutes. Transfer to a paper towel. Swirl some more oil in the same skillet and add the roasted peppers. Cook just until heated through, about 1 minute.

Add the beans, salt, and red pepper flakes to the pan and toss to combine. Top with the crispy prosciutto.

orangey basil beets

serves 4 to 6

The flavors of oranges and beets have a natural affinity for each other in a tart and sweet way. Pour the citrusy vinaigrette over the beets while they're still warm so the dressing flavors will be quickly absorbed.

3 large beets, scrubbed

Finely grated zest and juice (about ½ cup/120 mL) of 1 large orange

1 teaspoon red wine vinegar

¼ teaspoon coarse salt

Freshly ground black pepper

2 tablespoons extra-virgin olive oil

¼ cup (10 g) fresh basil leaves, roughly torn

Preheat the oven to 400°F (200°C). Wrap the beets in foil and roast until tender, about 1 hour. When cool enough to handle, peel the beets and cut into ¼-inch-thick (6 mm) slices. Spread the slices on a platter.

Meanwhile, whisk together the orange zest and juice, vinegar, salt, and a couple grinds of pepper. While whisking, slowly drizzle in the oil until thickened.

Pour the vinaigrette over the beets and scatter the basil leaves over the top.

WAYS WITH PREPPED AND PEELED BEETS

Once the beets are cooked, try any of these serving options:

Layer sliced beets on a platter with sliced ripe tomatoes. Dress with olive oil and salt.

Chop the beets into cubes and toss with a dash of white wine vinegar, a dollop of prepared horseradish, salt, a pinch of sugar, and chopped fresh dill.

Quarter the beets and top them with fresh goat cheese or sliced blue cheese and toasted walnuts.

italian fries

serves 6 (if you are very lucky)

Oven fries with an Italian twist! Everyone will go crazy for these, and there will never be enough.

6 or 7 Idaho potatoes, peeled and sliced into ⅓-inch-thick (8 mm) French fry–style strips (see Note), soaked in cold salted water

¼ cup (60 mL) extra-virgin olive oil

1 tablespoon dried Italian herbs or some combo of dried oregano, thyme, marjoram, and basil

2 cups (240 g) freshly grated Romano cheese

¼ cup (10 g) fresh parsley leaves, finely chopped

4 tablespoons (½ stick/57 g) salted butter, cut into 6 cubes

Coarse salt and freshly ground black pepper

Preheat the oven to 400°F (200°C).

Drain the potatoes and pat dry with paper towels. Spread 1 tablespoon of the olive oil on each of 2 rimmed baking sheets and spread out the potatoes. Overlapping is fine.

Sprinkle the dried herbs evenly over the potatoes. Liberally spread the cheese and parsley on top. Drizzle the remaining 2 tablespoons olive oil over the cheese. Scatter the cubed butter around the pans.

Bake until the potatoes are golden brown, rotating the pans after 30 minutes, 45 to 50 minutes total. Use a spatula to lift off the potatoes with all the crusty cheese adhered to them. Sprinkle with salt and pepper to taste. Serve hot.

NOTE

For a French-fry cut, peel the potatoes and slice lengthwise into ⅓-inch-thick (8 mm) slices. Stack the slices on top of one another, a few at a time, and slice lengthwise into ⅓-inch-thick (8 mm) strips. Peeled and sliced potatoes can turn brown pretty quickly. To avoid this, try floating the peeled, cut pieces in cold, salted water. When you're ready to cook, drain them and pat dry.

princely potatoes

serves 6

Truth be told, there isn't a health angle here. Sometimes, the mind/body just wants a dish of unapologetically fattening deliciousness—and that's where these potatoes, cooked in the classic "dauphinoise" style, come in. Serve with the Flat Roast Chicken (page 19).

3 pounds (1.4 kg) potatoes, such as russet, peeled and thinly sliced (about ⅛ inch/3 mm thick)

1 tablespoon unsalted butter, softened

2½ cups (600 mL) heavy cream

1½ cups (360 mL) whole milk

1 garlic clove, smashed

1¼ cups (5 ounces/142 g) shredded Gruyère cheese

1 teaspoon coarse salt

¼ teaspoon freshly ground white pepper

⅛ teaspoon freshly grated nutmeg

Put the peeled, sliced potatoes in a bowl of cold water. Preheat the oven to 350°F (180°C) with the rack in the center position. Spread the butter across the bottom and up the sides of a 2-quart (2 L) baking dish.

Bring the cream, milk, and garlic to a simmer in a saucepan. Drain the potatoes well and lay a quarter of them in the baking dish. Set aside a half cup (2 ounces/60 g) of the cheese. Scatter a quarter of the remaining cheese over the potatoes and top with a quarter each of the salt, white pepper, and nutmeg. Pour a quarter of the cream mixture over the potatoes to just cover. Repeat with the remaining ingredients to make a total of four layers. Cover with foil, set the baking dish on a rimmed baking sheet, and bake until tender and bubbly, 40 to 45 minutes.

Increase the oven temperature to 400°F (200°C). Uncover the pan and top with the reserved half cup (2 ounces/60 g) cheese. Bake, uncovered, until the cheese is melted and light golden brown, about 15 minutes. Remove the dish from the oven and let rest for at least 15 minutes before serving.

yorkshire pudding

makes 12

The secret to the highest, puffiest popovers is to have the batter at room temperature and to preheat the greased pan so that when the batter hits, the rise begins immediately (though you won't see it right away). Muffin tins will work just fine, but for the deepest, largest puffed beauties, get a popover pan.

4 large eggs, at room temperature

3¼ cups (780 mL) whole milk

2 cups (260 g) all-purpose flour

1½ teaspoons coarse salt

¼ teaspoon freshly ground black pepper

4 tablespoons (60 mL) pan drippings, reserved from the Standing Rib Roast (page 46)

Preheat the oven to 400°F (200°C). Place foil or a sheet pan below the rack you're using for the Yorkies to catch any overflow. Place the eggs, milk, flour, salt, and pepper in a blender and blend on high until the mixture is combined and resembles heavy cream. (This can be done several hours in advance.)

Pour 1 teaspoon pan drippings into each popover cup (half that amount if using a muffin tin). Heat in the oven for 2 minutes.

Quickly and carefully pour the batter into the cups, filling each about halfway. Put directly in the oven and do not open the door; keep the light on to watch what's going on in there! Bake until puffed and golden brown, about 30 minutes (the Yorkies will puff to the highest height, but not until the last 10 minutes of cooking time). Serve immediately.

DESSERTS

Best Chocolate Cake   Preheat oven 325°

1/2 tsp. salt
2 1/2 c. flour
1 1/2 tsp. Baking soda
1/2 cup cocoa

cinnamon
sugar

d Chocolate (opt.)
chopped
ilk

Butter

Chocolate Pudding

3 1/2 Tbs. flour
3   Tbs. Cocoa
    Salt (q.s.)
2 Tbs. butter
1 Egg (1)
1 1/2 cup milk
1 Tsp. vanilla
   sugar

so makes a good filling for Ch

Mix dry ing
Add milk - c
boiler till th
butter stir we
from fire - add
Egg - cook few m
1/2 cup chopped
be added if so d

apple crisp

serves 4 to 6

Satisfy any sweet tooth with a big, bubbling pan of a buttery, crisp-topped fruit dessert. If you're pie-shy, try this first. There's a lot of room for variation, and it doesn't require precision for success. Sliced fruit—pears or any type of stone fruit such as peach, plum, or nectarine work well—fills a buttered baking dish, and a quick topping is sprinkled on before it bakes.

FRUIT

2 tablespoons fresh lemon juice (about ½ large lemon)

4 apples, preferably 2 tart, such as Granny Smith, and 2 sweet, such as Mcintosh or Fuji

2 tablespoons granulated sugar

⅛ teaspoon ground cinnamon

¼ cup (33 g) all-purpose flour

2 tablespoons cold unsalted butter, cut into small pieces

TOPPING

¾ cup (62 g) rolled oats

½ cup (120 g) brown sugar, light or dark

¼ cup (29 g) walnuts or pecans, coarsely chopped

3 tablespoons all-purpose flour

½ teaspoon coarse salt

6 tablespoons (85 g) cold unsalted butter, cut into small pieces

OPTIONAL TOPPING ADD-INS

¼ teaspoon ground cinnamon

⅛ teaspoon ground ginger

⅛ teaspoon freshly ground black pepper

Pinch of nutmeg

Pinch of ground cloves

continued

Preheat the oven to 400°F (200°C). Position a rack in the center of the oven.

To prepare the fruit, place the lemon juice in a large bowl. Peel, core, and cut the apples into ½-inch (1 cm) wedges, tossing the pieces in the lemon juice as they are cut, to prevent browning.

To the apples, add the granulated sugar, cinnamon, and flour. Toss to combine and pour into a buttered 8 by 8-inch (20 by 20 cm) square or oval baking pan. Scatter the butter on top.

Make the topping in the same bowl. Combine the oats, brown sugar, nuts, flour, salt, and optional spices. Cut in the butter using a pastry blender, a fork, or two knives. Sprinkle the topping evenly over the fruit and bake on the center rack for 40 to 45 minutes, until the topping is dark golden and the apples are bubbling. Cool slightly on a wire cooling rack. Scoop out with a large spoon to serve in bowls.

dolly's chocolate bundt cake

makes 1 large cake

If you think you're just a competent or novice baker, this is the cake for you: it's easy to prepare, bakes in one pan, has a moist and tender texture, and requires only a glaze to finish. Its preparation is easy enough for a Sunday dinner, but its distinctive look is on the fancy side, which also makes it great for a birthday party or holiday table.

CAKE

1 cup (2 sticks/226 g) unsalted butter, softened

1½ cups (300 g) sugar

4 large eggs

1 teaspoon pure vanilla extract

2½ cups (325 g) all-purpose flour

½ cup (40 g) unsweetened cocoa powder

½ teaspoon ground cinnamon

1 teaspoon baking soda

1 teaspoon coarse salt

½ cup (85 g) chopped semisweet chocolate

½ cup (57 g) chopped walnuts (optional)

1 cup (240 mL) buttermilk

GLAZE

1 cup (170 g) finely chopped unsweetened chocolate

½ cup (100 g) sugar

⅓ cup (5 tablespoons plus one teaspoon/75 g) unsalted butter

⅔ cup (160 mL) heavy cream

2 tablespoons rum or brandy (optional)

Preheat the oven to 325°F (165°C). Butter a 12-cup (3 L) Bundt pan.

To make the cake, in a large bowl, cream together the butter and sugar. Beat in the eggs, one at a time, and then the vanilla. Scrape down the sides of the bowl.

In a separate bowl, whisk together the flour, cocoa, cinnamon, baking soda, and salt. Toss in the chopped chocolate and the walnuts, if using.

Into the butter mixture, alternately add the flour mixture and the buttermilk in three additions, ending with the flour. Mix just until everything is blended together; don't overmix.

Spoon the batter evenly into the Bundt pan and smooth the top of the batter. Bake for 55 to 60 minutes, or until a cake tester or toothpick

inserted into the cake comes out clean. Let the cake cool in the pan briefly. Turn out onto a cake plate to cool completely.

For the glaze, place a heatproof bowl over a pot of simmering water. Add the glaze ingredients and stir to melt and combine. Drizzle over the top of the cooled cake and let the glaze set, 15 to 20 minutes, before serving.

lemon soufflé pudding

Soufflés can be difficult to bake properly, but this imposter is a snap to make. A lemon-lover's favorite, this light and delicate dessert is a complementary finish to a rich and filling Sunday dinner. The bottom is silky and pudding-like while the top has a light meringue-type soufflé.

1 teaspoon unsalted butter, for the baking cups

5 large eggs, separated

¾ cup (150 g) sugar

1 tablespoon freshly grated lemon zest (about ½ large lemon)

¼ cup (60 mL) fresh lemon juice (about 1 large lemon)

2 tablespoons confectioners' sugar, for dusting

Whipped cream, for garnishing (optional)

Preheat the oven to 350°F (180°C). Using the teaspoon of butter, butter six (2-ounce/60 mL) baking cups or one 12-ounce/354 mL (8 by 10-inch/20 by 25 cm) oval baking dish. Place the cups or dish in a roasting pan. Bring a teakettle or medium pot of water to a boil.

Meanwhile, in a large bowl, beat the egg whites until stiff. In another clean bowl, beat the egg yolks until frothy and light in color, 3 to 4 minutes. Slowly add the sugar to the yolks while still beating. Mix in the lemon zest and juice.

Gently fold the egg whites into the egg yolk–lemon mixture. Pour the batter into each soufflé cup (filling each three-quarters full) or the baking dish. Put the roasting pan on the oven rack with the oven door open. Carefully and quickly pour the boiling water into the roasting pan to come halfway up the sides of the baking cups or dish. Slide the pan into the oven and bake for 20 to 25 minutes. Don't overcook.

Remove the pan from the oven. Set the cups or dish on a wire rack to cool. To serve, set the cups on serving plates or scoop from the baking dish into individual dishes. Dust with confectioners' sugar, then top with a dollop of whipped cream, if desired.

pumpkin flan

If pumpkin pie married caramel custard, their offspring would look like this pumpkin flan, which combines the best of both. It's a gorgeous and dramatic dessert that belies the ease with which it is made.

½ cup (100 g) granulated sugar

¾ cup (180 g) light brown sugar

½ teaspoon ground cinnamon

½ teaspoon ground ginger

¼ teaspoon ground nutmeg

¼ teaspoon coarse salt

1 cup (228 g) canned cooked pumpkin puree

1½ cups (360 mL) half-and-half or cream

5 large eggs, beaten

1 teaspoon pure vanilla extract

½ cup (120 mL) heavy cream, whipped (optional)

Preheat the oven to 350°F (180°C).

Put the granulated sugar in a 9-inch (23 cm) cake pan or pie plate, set on the center rack in the oven, and bake until the sugar is caramel colored, 8 to 12 minutes. Swirl to cover the bottom of the pie plate with the caramel.

In a large bowl, whisk together the brown sugar, cinnamon, ginger, nutmeg, and salt. Stir in the pumpkin puree. In a medium bowl, whisk together the half-and-half, eggs, and vanilla. Thoroughly blend the egg mixture into the pumpkin puree.

Set the pan in a large roasting pan and pour the custard over the caramel in the plate. Carefully pour enough hot tap water into the roasting pan to reach halfway up the sides of the pie plate. Bake until the custard is set, about 1 hour and 10 minutes. Cool and chill in the refrigerator. Run a knife around the outside edge of the flan and invert it onto a rimmed plate. Cut into wedges or scoop and serve, with a dollop of whipped cream, if desired.

strawberry rhubarb pie

makes one 9-inch (23 cm) pie with a lattice top
or with a double crust

Rhubarb alone is a pie that only purists covet. But rhubarb mixed with berries is a popular and flavorful combination of both tart and sweet. For this pie, raspberries, blueberries, blackberries, or cherries can be substituted for the strawberries. Serve the pie with a scoop of vanilla ice cream.

1 recipe Basic Pie Dough (see page 101)

3 cups (500 g) sliced strawberries

4 cups (400 g) sliced rhubarb

1½ cups (340 g) sugar, plus 2 teaspoons for sprinkling

½ cup (65 g) all-purpose flour, plus more for rolling out the dough

1¼ teaspoons coarse salt

2 tablespoons unsalted butter, cut into small pieces

1 large egg yolk

1 tablespoon milk

Preheat the oven to 425°F (220°C). Position the racks in the center of the oven and in the lower third.

On a well-floured surface, roll out one piece of dough to about 11 inches (28 cm) in diameter and lay it in the bottom of a 9-inch (23 cm) pie plate. Trim the edges of the dough flush with the edge of the pie plate's rim. Roll out the other piece of dough. Cut it into strips for a lattice crust, if desired, or leave intact.

In a large bowl, combine the strawberries, rhubarb, and the 1½ cups (340 g) sugar. Stir in the flour and salt, coating most of the fruit. Place the fruit in the dough-lined pie plate. Dot with the butter.

To make a lattice crust, lay half the strips of dough across in one direction, half in the other. Carefully weave them in and out of each other to create a basket-weave pattern. Or, lay the entire piece of dough over the filling to create a top crust. Trim the edges of the top crust or dough strips so they hang over the bottom crust by at least ¾ inch (2 cm). Tuck the top crust edges under the bottom crust

and roll under all around. Pinch together to close. Crimp the edges with your fingers or press with a fork. Chill the pie for a few minutes.

In a small bowl, whisk together the egg yolk and milk. If using an entire crust, cut slits in the top to allow steam to escape during baking. Brush the egg mixture evenly over the lattice or crust, being careful not to block the slits. Sprinkle with the remaining 2 teaspoons sugar.

Place a cookie sheet on the lower rack to catch any overflowing juices from the pie. Place the pie on the center rack and bake for 20 minutes, then reduce the heat to 400°F (200°C). Continue to bake until golden brown and cooked through, 50 to 60 more minutes. Cool on a wire cooling rack for 1 hour before serving.

basic pie dough

The milk in this recipe adds a touch more fat, which helps with the pliability and gives you a little more grace when rolling out the pie dough. Try making this both by hand and in a food processor; if you master both methods, you'll be ready to make pie regardless of what equipment—or lack thereof—is on hand. If you find yourself without a rolling pin, try a clean, dry wine or soda bottle, well floured, instead. Keep ingredients cold and work fast.

2 cups (255 g) all-purpose flour

1 teaspoon coarse salt

1 cup (2 sticks/227 g) very cold unsalted butter, cut into pieces

½ cup (125 mL) very cold milk or water

In a large bowl or in the bowl of a food processor, combine the flour and salt. Add the butter and cut in or pulse until the mixture resembles a coarse meal. Pour in the milk. Combine just until the dough holds together in a ball.

Turn the dough onto a piece of plastic wrap and lift the sides toward the middle to press them together. Cut the dough in half. Form each piece into a disk and wrap in plastic. Refrigerate for at least 15 minutes. If the dough has been refrigerated in advance, remove 15 minutes before using. The dough can be made and refrigerated for up to 3 days in advance or frozen for up to 6 weeks.

NOTE

To make the dough by hand, cut the butter into the flour with a fork, two knives, or a pastry cutter. Or, use your fingertips and work fast. Pour the milk over the fat/flour particles. Use your whole hand to gather everything together and form the dough. Handle as little as required to make a solid mass. The dough is right if a piece can be pinched together and hold its shape. Proceed to the second step.

boston cream pie

It's called pie, but let's face it, it's a cake—with an oozy, luscious pastry cream filling between moist cake layers with chocolate ganache dripping down the sides. A good way to tackle this cake is to make the cake layers and the pastry cream in advance. When ready to assemble, make the ganache topping.

CAKE

2½ cups (325 g) all-purpose flour
½ teaspoon baking powder
½ teaspoon baking soda
1 teaspoon coarse salt
1 cup (240 mL) safflower oil
1½ cups (300 g) sugar
4 large eggs, at room temperature
1 teaspoon pure vanilla extract
1 cup (242 g) sour cream

PASTRY CREAM

1 large egg
4 large egg yolks
⅓ cup (67 g) sugar
¼ cup (33 g) all-purpose flour
1½ cups (360 mL) whole milk, heated
½ teaspoon pure vanilla extract

TOPPING

1⅓ cups (8 ounces/227 g) semisweet chocolate, finely chopped
1 cup (240 mL) heavy cream, hot

For the cake, preheat the oven to 350°F (180°C) with a rack in the center position. Oil and flour two 8-inch (20 cm) round cake pans. Whisk together the flour, baking powder, baking soda, and salt in a medium bowl.

Whisk together the oil and sugar in a large bowl. Whisk in the eggs and vanilla. Add the flour mixture in 3 additions, alternating with the sour cream in 2 additions (beginning and ending with the flour). Divide the batter between the prepared pans.

Bake for 30 to 35 minutes, until the cakes pull away from the sides of the pans. Cool the pans on a wire rack for 10 minutes, then remove from the pans to cool completely, right-side up.

continued

For the pastry cream, lightly beat the egg and yolks together in the bowl of a stand mixer fitted with the paddle attachment or in a large bowl using a hand mixer. Add the sugar a little at a time and continue beating until the mixture falls in ribbons when the beater is lifted, about 5 minutes. Mix in the flour, then add the milk in a steady stream.

Transfer the mixture to a saucepan, bring just to a boil, and boil gently over medium heat, whisking, until the mixture thickens, 8 to 10 minutes. Strain the pastry cream through a fine sieve into a large bowl. Stir in the vanilla. Press plastic wrap against the surface. Cool for at least 1 hour.

For the chocolate ganache topping, put the chocolate in a medium bowl. Pour the cream over it and leave undisturbed for 1 minute. Stir gently, until the chocolate is melted and smooth. Let cool for 10 minutes.

Slice off the domed top of 1 cake layer to level it. With your fingers, remove some of the cake to make a ½-inch (1 cm) hollow, leaving a ½-inch (1 cm) border around the edge. Place on a cake stand or plate. Fill with the pastry cream. Top with the second cake layer, domed-side up. Pour the topping over the cake, letting it run down the sides. Chill for at least 5 hours or as long as overnight before serving.

new york–style cheesecake

serves 12

"New York–style" means heavy on cream—sour cream and cream cheese—for a decadent, swoonworthy cheesecake. The trick is to cook it enough to set without cracking the top. And don't cheat on the chill time.

CRUST

7½ (4 ounces/113 g) graham crackers, broken into pieces

⅓ cup (67 g) sugar

¼ teaspoon coarse salt

4 tablespoons (57 g) unsalted butter, melted

FILLING

2½ pounds (1.1 kg) cream cheese, or 5 (8-ounce/227 g) packages, at room temperature

8 tablespoons (1 stick/113 g) unsalted butter, at room temperature

1 (8-ounce/227 g) container sour cream, at room temperature

1¾ cups (350 g) sugar

5 large eggs

2 large egg yolks

Grated zest of 1 lemon (about 2 tablespoons)

1 teaspoon pure vanilla extract

Preheat the oven to 375°F (190°C) with a rack in the lower-third position. Butter a 9-inch (23 cm) springform pan. Line the sides of the pan with 4-inch-wide (10 cm) strips of parchment and butter the parchment.

For the crust, pulse the graham crackers, sugar, and salt to fine crumbs in a food processor. Add the butter and pulse until fully incorporated. Press the mixture evenly onto the bottom of the prepared pan. Bake for 15 minutes, or until the crust is golden brown and set. Transfer the pan to a wire rack to cool for 10 minutes. (Leave the oven on.)

For the cheesecake, in the bowl of a large stand mixer or in a large bowl with a hand mixer, beat the cream cheese, butter, sour cream, and sugar until light and smooth. Beat in the whole eggs one at a time,

until fully incorporated. Beat in the egg yolks, zest, and vanilla extract.

Crisscross two 18-inch-long (46 cm) pieces of foil. Put the springform pan in the center of the foil and wrap the foil tightly around the bottom and sides of the pan to create a watertight seal. Transfer to a roasting pan. Pour the filling into the springform pan and smooth the top.

Pour enough boiling water into the roasting pan to come halfway up the sides of the springform pan and carefully transfer to the oven. Bake for about 1 hour and 15 minutes, or until the top of the cheesecake is golden brown and the edges are set but the center still jiggles slightly. Remove from the oven and allow the cheesecake to stand in the water bath for 1 hour.

Lift the cheesecake from the water bath and remove the foil and parchment. Chill the cheesecake for at least 8 hours and up to 24 hours.

To serve, remove the sides of the springform pan and the parchment strips. Cut the cheesecake with a long thin-bladed knife.

oatmeal chocolate chip cookies

Given the choice of only one cookie to eat, many of us would go for old-fashioned chocolate chip cookies. In this recipe, oatmeal adds texture and a healthy ingredient, which makes these cookies an excellent pick for a family dessert.

¾ cup (98 g) all-purpose flour

½ teaspoon baking soda

¾ teaspoon coarse salt

8 tablespoons (1 stick/113 g) unsalted butter, softened, plus more for the pans

6 tablespoons (75 g) granulated sugar

6 tablespoons (90 g) light brown sugar

1 large egg

½ teaspoon pure vanilla extract

¼ teaspoon water

1 cup (83 g) rolled oats

1 cup (6 ounces/170 g) semisweet chocolate chips

Preheat the oven to 375°F (190°C). Butter or line 2 rimmed baking sheets.

In a small bowl, whisk together the flour, baking soda, and salt.

In a large bowl, beat together the butter, sugars, egg, vanilla, and water. Add the flour mixture and stir to combine. Stir in the oats and chocolate chips.

Drop by teaspoonfuls onto the baking sheets, spacing the dough 1 inch (3 cm) apart. Bake for 10 to 12 minutes, until lightly golden in color. Remove to cooling racks.

INDEX

Note: Page numbers in *italics* refer to illustrations.

Library of Congress Cataloging-in-Publication Data is on file.

ISBN 978-1-57965-936-3

Cover and book design adapted from Jennifer S. Muller and Erica Heitman-Ford

Artisan books are available at special discounts when purchased in bulk for premiums and sales promotions as well as for fund-raising or educational use. Special editions or book excerpts also can be created to specification. For details, contact the Special Sales Director at the address below, or send an e-mail to specialmarkets@workman.com.

For speaking engagements, contact speakersbureau@workman.com.

Published by Artisan
A division of Workman Publishing Co., Inc.
225 Varick Street
New York, NY 10014-4381
artisanbooks.com

Artisan is a registered trademark of Workman Publishing Co., Inc.

This book has been adapted from *Mad Hungry: Feeding Men and Boys* (Artisan, 2009), *Mad Hungry Cravings* (Artisan, 2013), and *Mad Hungry Family* (Artisan, 2016).

Published simultaneously in Canada by Thomas Allen & Son, Limited

Printed in China

First printing, July 2019

10 9 8 7 6 5 4 3 2 1